AF334569

From Paris I Came

i

FROM PARIS I CAME

Dr. Bobbi Lancaster

FROM PARIS I CAME

From Paris I Came

This book is dedicated to my mother, in celebration of her ninetieth birthday.

From Paris I Came

FROM PARIS I CAME

WRITTEN BY
DR. BOBBI LANCASTER

COVER DESIGN AND LAYOUT BY
JACKIE CASEY

EDITING AND PHOTOGRAPHY BY
LUCY LANCASTER

ALSO BY DR. BOBBI LANCASTER:

THE RED LIGHT RUNNER

PUTTING DOWN ROOTS

MY FRIEND FLUTTER

BACKYARD ADVENTURES

From Paris I Came

TABLE OF CONTENTS

From Paris I Came

From Paris I Came

PROLOGUE

I thought I knew everything there was to know about my ninety year old mother. However, just the other day, her reply to an everyday question caught me off guard. The response was nonchalant and assumed I was aware of this private part of her life. Her answer left me wondering: who is this woman? How could I have not known? Perhaps I'd become so accustomed to calling her Mom that I had failed to see her as a real person. I was well aware that children can put on blinders when it comes to looking at their parents. We can't begin to picture them when they were young and doing crazy things.

It was at that moment I remembered a file I started years ago. It contained hastily scribbled notes concerning stories my mother had told me. I was going to write a book about her adventures, and then something got in the way. Perhaps now was the time. Her ninetieth birthday was five weeks away and I imagined she would be thrilled to reminisce about old memories. And then I recalled why I had abandoned the project.

It is a difficult undertaking to write about a person's past, especially when you know they are going to read the story very carefully. And not all events were necessarily pleasant. Their story intersects with other individuals too, who may prefer to remain hidden and this adds to the challenge. Maybe I might agitate a hornet's nest and the end result would be arguments about the truth, defensiveness, and hurt feelings.

However, the more I thought about it, the more I became convinced of its merits. The book would be an opportunity to document a moment in Canadian history, to educate about the trials and tribulations of a family-run farm, to emphasize the importance of a mentor, and to memorialize the real and authentic life of my mother.

I had more questions to ask, given her new revelation, and I still had to find that old file. There was no time to waste given her rapidly approaching special day.

CHAPTER ONE
LAWRENCE WELK

The highway to Boyce Thompson Arboretum was empty of cars as I made my way to another general tour. The sun was peaking over the Superstition Mountains and caused me to squint and fumble for sunglasses. I loved my work as a docent at this cherished state park. Connecting visitors to nature had become my most recent passion.

The stoplight at Peralta Trail was the cue to call my mother. Our phone conversations while I drove to the park had become a ritual. And in the early morning hours, she was guaranteed to be in her room at the assisted living facility she now called home. My hands free phone dialed her number as the cactus-studded scenery whizzed by.

"Hello," she said in her usual hesitant, somewhat apprehensive manner.

"Hi Mom…it's me…Bobbi…what are you up to?"

"Oh Bobbi, it's so good to hear your voice. Give me a minute while I turn the television down. You caught me dancing. Alright, I can hear you now"

"What do you mean I caught you dancing? Who are you dancing with?"

"Nobody…I just dance alone"

"How long has this been going on?"

"I've done this for years. When I can find reruns of the Lawrence Welk show, I stand up and dance—all by myself. Now that I'm old, I simply sway side to side because I don't want to lose my balance and topple over."

I was surprised that Mom had never shared this touching information with me before. In an instant, I felt closer to her and a new door had opened. I wondered if she had shared this personal revelation with my sister and brothers too.

The past several years, it takes much longer to have a conversation with Mom. She has significant word finding difficulties, causing her much frustration. Next week she is going to the doctor to see if a medication can improve her speech.

Many questions about dancing and other things were now twirling in my head. But this was not the time and place to begin that discussion.

We were commenting on the weather when, quite abruptly, she exclaimed that the Lawrence Welk show was almost over. Mom wanted to enjoy one more dance. And then she hung up.

The phone and everything around me became silent. I could picture her moving back and forth—eyes closed—alone with her thoughts as she swayed to the music.

From Paris I Came

CHAPTER TWO
FROM PARIS I CAME

Rosalie Clara Robert was born at Saint Joseph's Hospital in Chatham, Ontario on November 5, 1929. She was later told her much anticipated delivery occurred late in the day, just before midnight. Rosalie was the third child for Alphy and Anna Robert—French Canadian farmers—scratching out a hardscrabble life for themselves and their other daughters: Rita and Jane. The stock market had crashed the week before and they were hoping for a boy.

Rita had been born at home five years earlier. With his wife in labor and without a home telephone, Alphy ran two miles to a neighboring farm to call the doctor. Apparently the nightmarish delivery was assisted by Anna's mother, who lived on a farm not far away. The doctor eventually arrived—late—and was greeted by the lusty cry of new life. Rita became the celebrated and indulged first child for this young couple.

Jane arrived in 1927 and this time, the Roberts sought the safety and accepted the expense of a hospital setting. Fingers were crossed that the second child would be a boy. What they received instead was the heart and soul of this household. Jane proved to be an energetic fireplug: a prankster; the outspoken one; an athlete with a ready laugh and a wild spirit.

Of course Rosalie arrived two years later—a third daughter on a hundred acre farm—the disappointment was palpable. As the endless crop and livestock chores continued, she represented just another mouth to feed.

Her first memory was of being reprimanded when she was two years old, because she was crying. The scolding devolved into nonsensical spanking because she could not be quieted.

It was Rita who came to her rescue. She discovered the cause of Rosalie's distress—a boil—on the inside of her right upper arm. This necessitated a visit to the doctor, a minor operation and yet another expense related to this unnecessary daughter.

The Roberts were finally blessed with a son—Gerry—in 1932 during the Great Depression. This golden child was coddled from the very beginning. It was assumed he would be a hard worker and the future of the farm would be in his hands.

Rosalie remembers being a fearful young child: scared of the dark; frightened to be alone; terrified of birds, butterflies and other fluttering things; petrified of her father. What triggered these fears?

Perhaps it stemmed from being left alone in the living room with the body of her deceased grandfather. This incident occurred during his wake, when the mourners exited the house and accidentally left her locked inside.

Maybe it started when Rita and Jane thought it was funny to release a butterfly down the front of her dress. The insect frantically tried to regain its freedom as it crawled and flapped against Rosalie's skin.

Possibly it was caused by listening to her father's raised, angry voice and then subsequently witnessing her mother's bruises and broken wrist.

She recalls sensing danger when her father was near.

Or maybe it was the time she was alone and playing quietly in her second floor bedroom. Suddenly a ghost appeared, dressed in white and Rosalie was terrified. She fought for her life and pulled the bed sheet off the perpetrator. It was her sister, Jane, now grimacing from a bleeding scalp wound as Rosalie held a clump of black hair in her clenched right hand.

To say the least, Rosalie did not experience a secure and happy early childhood. However, everything changed one day when, at five years of age, she was dropped off at her maternal grandmother Belanger's farmhouse. Rosalie called her *memere*. They were alone and something truly magical was about to occur.

Her grandmother was quite musical and played several instruments, including the piano. She wanted to teach her granddaughter how to dance and choreographed a skit. Rosalie was told to stand at the top of the staircase and announce, in her loudest voice, "From Paris I came. Rosalie is my name."

She was then instructed to descend the stairs to the landing, while her grandmother played a tune. The landing became Rosalie's stage. She performed the jig and danced until she lost her breath. And she smiled and smiled and her heart burst with happiness. They rehearsed the routine—over and over. She became giddy from the exertion, ran to her grandmother and hugged her for the longest time.

She left Memere Belanger's home and experienced an unfamiliar sensation called confidence. She felt loved, valued and respected. Her life mattered and this knowledge was intoxicating

Rosalie had become a dancer, she was from Paris, and her future was bright.

From Paris I Came

CHAPTER THREE
JOAN OF ARC

The Robert family moved into their newly built, white, two-story farm house on the Bear Line: a dirt road that connected the tiny francophone village of Paincourt with the suburbs of English speaking Chatham. The road was straight and easy to navigate. Connecting the two cultures it brought together proved to be much more challenging.

A gleaming red barn stood proudly in the yard behind the house. There were horses that helped plow the fields, pigs for their bacon and cows for their milk and cream. Numerous cats took up residence and kept the mice in check. And a dog named Rex ferociously guarded the property and chased the passing cars and their clouds of dust. He lunged at the spinning tires. His was the most dangerous job, and Rex was replaced by another Rex and later a Rover too. These dogs were no match for the speeding automobiles.

Prominently displayed on the side of the barn that faced the road, in big white letters, was the statement of ownership—Alphy Robert and Son. Of course there was no mention of Anna or the three girls. It was definitely a sign from a different time.

It appears that Rosalie did engage in carefree play, albeit briefly. She played house in an unused corn crib with her cousin Marguerite, skipped rope, shot basketballs, learned how to hopscotch, enjoyed sleigh rides, feasted at corn roasts and rescued baby kittens.

However, by the age of six, she joined Rita and Jane and they performed men's work together: suckering tobacco, baling hay, hoeing weeds in rows of corn as far as the eye could see. And there were chickens to feed, eggs to collect, and tomatoes to pick that stained their hands an embarrassing green. Gerry was a toddler and not able to help yet.

When the outdoor work was done, the men rested and enjoyed their big meals and a beer or three. This is still referred to as male privilege. However, the daughters' housework had just begun. They joined their mother and prepared the food, set the table, washed dishes, laundered work clothes, emptied chamber pots, separated milk and churned butter. And all this was accomplished in a primitive setting, initially without electricity or a toilet. The outhouse was near the boundary fence to the south of the house.

In early September, 1935, Rosalie joined her sisters on the long walk to Saint Bernard SS 13. It was her first day of attendance at this one-room French school, and four teachers provided lessons from grade one to eight. Rosalie was understandably nervous. However, her confidence and self-belief were being propped up by frequent visits to her grandmother's house. Rosalie's poise was soon to be tested.

During the first week of classes, she raised her hand to obtain permission—she urgently needed a bathroom break. The teacher was her aunt, Dorothy Martin. She thought Rosalie was volunteering to answer a question and sent her to the blackboard. Rosalie protested, crossed her legs and danced uncomfortably— the original jig. The teacher ignored the histrionics and continued the lesson.

The inevitable happened. A puddle of pee gathered around her feet as Rosalie gazed at the floor—a piece of chalk still firmly held in her hand. It was Lionel Faubert, a grade eight student, who noticed it first and his mocking laugh reverberated off all four walls. His jubilation was short-lived: he was ordered by his teacher to clean up the mess while Rosalie ran to the bathroom to change clothes.

As an aside, Rosalie and Lionel met many years later and shared a hearty laugh about the incident that had linked them forever in time.

In the blink of an eye, it was time for Christmas break and Rosalie remembered two presents as if she opened them yesterday. The first was a doll that she treasured, until she met a girl at school who had received no presents—they were destitute. So Rosalie did what came natural to her: she gave the doll to her poor friend.

The second present came from her grandmother Belanger. It was a pair of tap shoes. The two of them continued to meet and Memere taught Rosalie some real dance steps. She also curled Rosalie's hair for special occasions—like First Communion—and created outfits for her too.

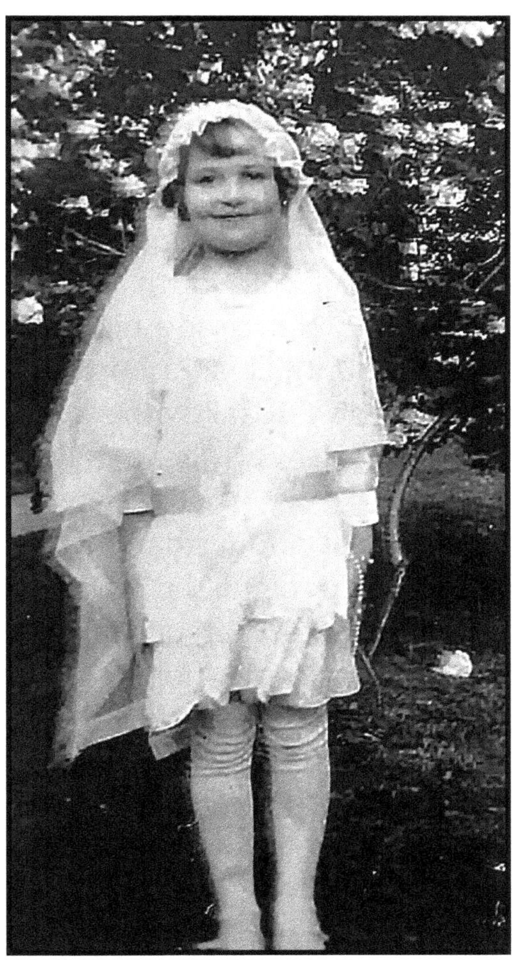

She was the best dressed girl at school along with Jane, who was also the recipient of Memere's love and seamstress skills.

Rosalie blossomed under her grandmother's watchful eye, became an honor student and participated in public speaking contests called declamations.

The grade school years raced by and she experienced incredible teachers along the way. Mr. Mozart Emory taught her grades three and four and then his brother, Alphy, replaced him for grades five, six and seven. They were both inspirational and demanding. Her grade eight teacher was another aunt, Lina Robert, and she bestowed upon Rosalie the crowning achievement of her early academic life.

Before I tell you about that momentous event, I want to highlight several other formative incidents that occurred during this period of time. When Rosalie was nine years old, she traveled to the big city of Chatham with her parents and Jane. They were shopping and of course, they were speaking French. There were several boys who spied the country bumpkins and mocked them because of their dress and accents. Rosalie felt ashamed and became quiet. However, true to form, Jane dished it right back and told them where to go.

When they returned home, Rosalie and Jane agreed on a new goal: they would learn how to speak English. They obtained a dictionary that translated from French to English and read it over and over. And with the help of a cousin who lived in Chatham—Ralph West—they became bilingual. It was one of the most difficult challenges either one of them ever embraced.

Rosalie also discovered a new place to dance apart from her memere's home. Every Friday night, the farm community would congregate at a hall—a converted barn—in the town of Paincourt. Her parents went frequently and Jane and Rosalie tagged along. Rita often remained home because she was tired. They would watch the grown-ups dance and memorize their routines. Then they would take to the floor and perfect the steps until everyone paused for a meal at eleven.

Rosalie was in her element. Her memere was in attendance too and nodded her approval. Rosalie did not want to stop: she had succumbed to the excitement and was a slave to the beat.

Another incident occurred during the elementary school years and it had nothing to do with school or dance. One of Rosalie's favorite barnyard cows—yes, they became pets—was pregnant and the delivery was complicated. The veterinarian was not available and Grandmother Belanger arrived on the scene. She had no formal training. However, she was an expert in supporting others and helping them attain goals they never thought possible. Memere exhorted the cow, made several suggestions and the calf was born without injury. It was miraculous. Was there anything her grandmother couldn't do?

Rosalie did not know that grade eight would be her final year of formal education. She had plans to become a nurse. She did not realize that the school play would be her swan song.

There were auditions and the question of who would be chosen to play Joan of Arc remained in the balance. Rosalie was not the most popular girl. However, her memere had groomed her well. Dancing had allowed her to experience mastery, grow in confidence, and learn the value of determination and hard work.

Rosalie was awarded the role and she literally became the most fearless Joan of Arc during the next several months of rehearsals. The play was entered in a competition against six other schools.

Her parents were not present when Rosalie gave the performance of her life: apparently a pregnant mare was in labor. Their seats were still empty when she was announced as Best Actress. If they had been in attendance to witness Rosalie's triumphant achievement, they might have made a different choice about her future.

In every life, there are the highest of highs and the gut-wrenching lows. Rosalie wanted to continue her studies and Grandmother Belanger had arranged for relatives—a childless couple in California—to take her in and allow this Joan of Arc to soar to new heights. However, Rosalie's father was a firm believer that higher education for women was a waste of time. He had other plans for his youngest daughter: she had to go to work and help sustain the family.

There was no point in asking her mother to intervene. Anna was a good person: clever, hard-working, honest, humble, and once upon a time, she could play the piano like her mother. Anna had been given five thousand dollars by her parents to help start her new life with Alphy. This wedding present paid for the barn that did not bear her name and it paid for the house too. Somewhere in the process, Anna had become diminished and incapable of influencing her husband's mind. She had been silenced.

The decision was final: there would be no more school. Rosalie's fate was sealed and her relationship with her father was dealt a fatal blow.

CHAPTER FOUR
THE CHERRY TREE

23

The small suitcase was packed. Rosalie regarded her fourteen year old face in the mirror, smoothed her hair and walked confidently to the waiting truck. She would never call the farm house her home again.

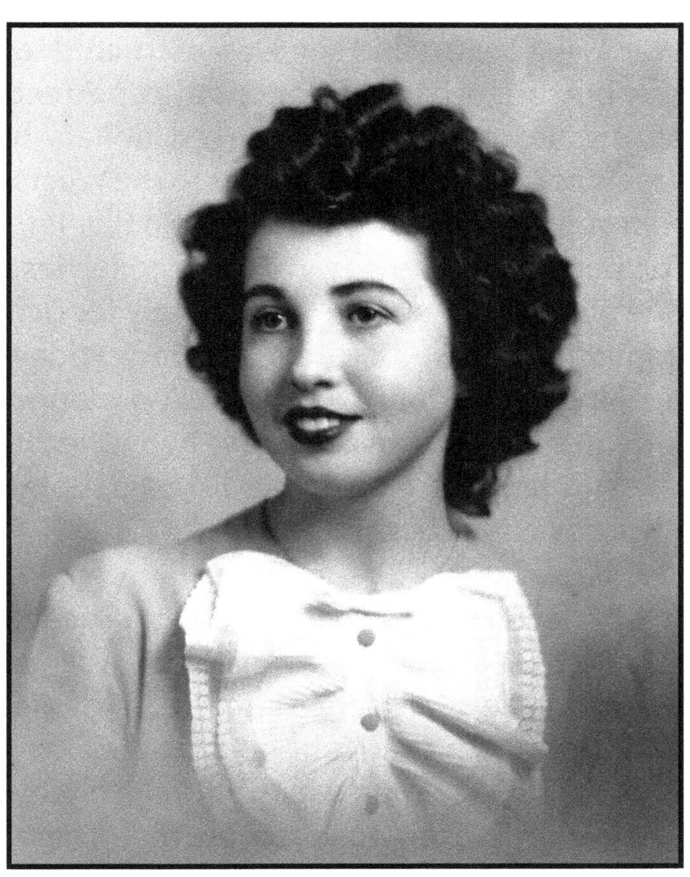

Arrangements had been made for her to live in Chatham with her father's sister, Aunt Irene West, and her husband, Uncle Goldie. They had two children: Ralph, who had helped her learn English, and Roseanne. Jane was already living there.

Rosalie started work the next week at the American Pad and Textile factory. This company was making uniforms for World War Two soldiers and she was instructed to sew buttons on shirts and construct perfect seams. Rosalie was paid seven dollars a week, of which six dollars went to the Wests for room and board. She had one dollar left for personal expenses including toiletries. She put ten cents aside immediately for her admission to the barn dance every Friday evening in Paincourt. There was no money left over to send back home, but at least she and Jane were no longer listed in Alphy Robert's expense column.

Her benevolent boss was Mr. Weatherhead. Rosalie's immediate supervisor was a woman called Millicent Lancaster. Rosalie had never met anyone quite like her: officious, stern, mean-spirited, and bitchy were words used to describe her. There was tension between the two of them right from the beginning.

Millicent's son, Doug, visited his mother frequently at the factory and he apparently took notice of Rosalie. He was three years older and rather shy. No words were exchanged.

Not long into her employment, Rosalie became the object of Millicent's explosive temper. She inspected an entire day of Rosalie's work, deemed it unacceptable and ripped all the buttons off the shirts. Mr. Weatherhead witnessed the tirade and took the now sobbing farm girl aside. He re-assigned her to the time office. Rosalie was free from the witch—or so she thought.

There was only one thing that made her life bearable: the weekly dance back home. She and Jane would arrange a ride to and from the West's home. The barn was packed: parents on the dance floor, single boys leaning against one wall, girls in pretty dresses lined up on the other, babies crying, and a local band belting out the current hits.

There was not a moment to waste: the two of them jumped into the action and whirled around the floor. By now Rosalie was proficient at every step: foxtrot, jitterbug, waltz, two-step, and polka. She especially liked to square dance.

One evening a cousin, Oscar Bechard, approached Rosalie and told her a friend of his wanted to meet her. She followed Oscar outside and his friend could not be found. After a brief search, he was located high in a cherry tree—drunk—he'd climbed it on a dare. This friend jumped down from his perch and introduced himself. His name was Doug Lancaster—Millicent's son—and he wanted to dance with her. He persisted and followed Rosalie inside where he proceeded to step on her feet and display absolutely no dancing ability.

Jane observed what was going on and intervened. She walked up to Doug, asked him to dance, stomped on his foot, and then turned and walked away. She had made her point, as usual.

Several weeks later, Millicent approached Rosalie at work and was as sweet as can be. She informed Rosalie that Doug had been hurt and wanted to see her. Millicent insisted and Rosalie went to the Lancaster home on Park Avenue West where she met Doug. He had a job at Libby's and a box of canned peas had fallen on his head and broken his nose. His face was swollen like a balloon and she offered him sympathy.

Doug was obviously smitten. He secretly followed her home from work one day and saw her disappear into a residence at 46 Richmond Street. He wanted to ask Rosalie for a date but lacked the courage to approach her face to face. A phone call would be easier.

Doug found a phone book and looked for that Richmond Street address. Of course he started with the A's. It was a laborious job: thousands of people lived in Chatham. He would have to comb through the entire book until he reached the W's and found the Wests' number.

His heart was pounding when he placed the call. Mrs. West picked up the phone but did not recognize who was calling and hung up. This happened repeatedly and Doug would have to find another way.

Several weeks later at another Paincourt dance, Doug reintroduced himself to

Rosalie. He was sober, clean shaven and displayed good manners. She noted that he was actually quite handsome.

That evening, she taught him the foxtrot and they talked. Rosalie learned about his bout with polio and his beloved dog, Mickey. She visited the Park Avenue West home again: met his sister, Marlene; chatted with his father, Lorne; looked at his model airplane collection and discovered that Millicent was actually quite friendly and musically inclined too—she played the organ.

Of course he learned about Rosalie's story too. They went to the movie theater and enjoyed picnics as well—just the two of them. She was impressed he was not pushy about things like sex. He knew nothing about her Roman Catholic faith and she knew even less about Protestants.

Everything was moving almost too quickly for Rosalie now. Doug told her he felt compelled to enlist in the United States military and represent his country of birth— he had been born in Detroit. He wanted to fight the Japanese and defend freedom everywhere. She admired his passion but feared for the safety of her new best friend. Doug enlisted in October of 1944 and they promised to exchange letters as often as possible. And then he was off to become a paratrooper—a certain death sentence.

At about the same time, Jane fell in love with Hubert Doyle—Doc—a farm boy from Raleigh. It was a match made in heaven and they eventually married and moved to Detroit where work was more readily available.

Rita had married Ernest King from Paincourt and she assumed the life of a farmer's wife, just like her mother.

Rosalie continued to work at the textile company. She returned at the end of each day to tension in the West home. Uncle Goldie's father was now living with them. He had advanced dementia and spent his days chewing tobacco and spitting in a spittoon, and everywhere else. When he wasn't spitting, he alternated between calm and combative—severely scratching Aunt Irene's face during a moment of panic.

Doug sent her daily correspondence—love letters—in which he would talk about fear and about a future with her.

It was dancing that kept her sane and allowed her to cope with being alone in the world. A new hall had opened in Chatham at the Masonic temple. Rosalie went as often as she could. Big bands were booked at the venue and they played her favorite songs. Jane attended until she moved away and Rosalie enjoyed dancing with Wilfred King, Rita's brother-in-law. He could really dance and was smart too—he had plans to go to McGill University. There was certainly an attraction.

However, she had promised to wait for Doug.

From time to time, Johnny—the Zoot Suitor—would ask her to dance. He was the most talented partner she ever had. He twirled her about the floor and lifted her above his head. People stepped back and watched as they accelerated around the hall at a dizzying pace. It was dangerous and exhilarating all at the same time.

The war ended and Doug was discharged in August of 1946. Rosalie had a big decision to make.

CHAPTER FIVE
TOMATO PICKING

Doug returned to a hero's welcome. The Second World War was over, the Great Depression was a fading memory and the future was bright. He had a tattoo with her name on his arm and he was smoking now like everyone else. Rosalie thought it was fashionable and started smoking too.

He wanted to marry her. A decision had to be made. Wilfred King had left for university in Montreal, and Goldie's father was still spitting chew tobacco everywhere. Rosalie's father hated this city-slicker named Doug—but since when did his opinion matter—and her mother had no opinion. Grandmother Belanger told her to follow her heart—and she did.

Wedding bans—a promise of marriage—between Douglas Lorne Lancaster and Rosalie Clara Robert were published. They continued to go to dances at the Masonic temple. Doug's grandfather checked tickets at the door and Wilf Lancaster and his band—Doug's uncle—were often the featured entertainment. They fell in love dancing to tunes by Benny Goodman, Guy Lombardo and Artie Shaw.

Rosalie remained at the textile factory and Doug found a bookkeeper job. She prayed that she'd made the correct decision. September 11, 1948 was chosen as the wedding date. Rosalie dreamed of a big family with six children.

She quit her job the week of the wedding. The day before, there was an urgent call from Alphy. He was short-staffed, there was a bumper crop of ripening tomatoes and they had to be picked right away.

Rosalie responded, believing she might win the affection of her disapproving father. She gathered the fruit until her hands became raw and they were stained green for added measure.

Her wedding ceremony failed to live up to expectations. Doug was physically ill— an asthma attack and sinusitis. Her father arrived after a night of drinking and the usual morning chores. He made a farce of the event in front of the small number of attendees—he was drunk. Millicent and her mother, Anna, had managed to purchase the same dress for the event—an embarrassment for both. The reception at the Blue Bird Restaurant was underwhelming.

Doug and Rosalie spent their wedding night in London, Ontario. His asthma attack was severe and he could hardly breathe. The next morning, they embarked on a two day honeymoon to Niagara Falls in a black '32 Chevy. Several flat tires and breakdowns later, they returned to Chatham to start their new life.

There were so many bad omens but Rosalie kept saying to herself that everything was going to be alright. She had her doubts.

CHAPTER SIX
THE BOILING POT

The announcement of new life is always exciting. Mom was expecting, and the baby was me. Everyone was thrilled, especially Millicent, because I would be her first grandchild. My mom ate well and stopped smoking—she was looking out for me from the very beginning. As her pregnancy progressed, complications including hypertension and fluid retention developed. She was instructed to rest and keep her stress levels down. The young couple was in the process of moving to a new home on Park Avenue West—across from Dad's parents. And then the unimaginable happened.

On June 17, 1950, the police knocked on her door. They informed her that Dad had been arrested for sexual assault and he was in jail. The news spread like a wildfire. This had to be a mistake.

Apparently he had visited the wife of a friend named Billy King, who had recently been incarcerated for another matter. Dad went to their home to offer help. One thing led to another and she called the police. Now he was behind bars and unable to make bail. His parents were mortified.

Jane arrived to help her sister. Mom went into labor and I was delivered—after a long struggle and anesthesia—on June 23, 1950. My father's parents posted bail and Dad barely made it to the hospital to welcome me into the world.

What a mess!

The doctors kept us in hospital for a few days. We arrived at our new home and it resembled a disaster scene: unpacked boxes, dirty dishes, unwashed laundry, and garbage everywhere.

My mother resurrected her old Joan of Arc performance. She stood tall, expected nothing from anyone and moved forward. There was no time for dancing at the moment.

Dad finally made an embarrassing appearance: his apology was accepted, promises were made, the legal mess was sorted out, and Mom tried to put the incident out of her mind. This fragile young family careened into the future, knowing that everything could be lost in an instant.

Mom devoted all her energy toward Dad and me. He found a better paying bookkeeper job, they made new friends and sometimes left me alone with Millicent and Lorne across the street—Nana and Grandpa to me.

They went dancing and Mom became lost in the melody all over again, at least for a little while.

I'd like to think that Mom gathered me from my crib when I was fussing at night. She'd hold me tight and dance around the room to calm the two of us down. I'm not certain this ever happened, but it is a pleasant thought nevertheless.

Dad would drive the two of us to church every Sunday. I received a Catholic baptism because this was of paramount importance to Mom. My father would pick us up after the service. Attending church was not a priority for him.

They were both smoking and Dad was drinking heavily at times. He had moments of easy frustration and developed a temper. Something was simmering below the surface and he did not want to talk about it.

The daily routine was broken by another happy announcement—Mom was pregnant again. She delivered my new baby brother, Ron, on October 11, 1952. He peed on me during one of his first diaper changes, but I loved him all the same. Mom was ecstatic—Dad not so much. He was concerned about how to pay for the added expense. The pressure was building.

I was small and had not started school yet, but it did not stop me from helping mom change Ron's diapers, dust, vacuum the house, hang clothes on the line, and wash the car. I used a ladder to reach the windshield and fell, breaking my arm in the

the winter.

The bills were endless: Sandy could not wear Ron and my hand-me-downs; we all had poor teeth but mine were the worst; I required hospitalization and almost died after a botched, ether-assisted tonsillectomy.

Mom found part-time work cleaning houses and doing laundry and ironing for a professional lady up the street.

And then Dad snapped again. His verbal and physical abuse was usually alcohol fueled, and Ron and Mom were his favorite targets. He hit me only once that I remember—in the head—when I tried to protect my mother from his blows. I was around seven and I think I was concussed, because my mind went blank.

This cycle of violence repeated many times throughout their married life. Between these episodes, there was always a tension. One never knew what might trigger him. My mother was not doing the jitterbug anymore. Now she was dancing on proverbial eggshells, trying to keep the peace.

Mom would gaze at him at times when he was busy: building a butterfly net and display cases for my insect collection; creating an ice rink in the backyard in bone-chilling conditions where the kids could learn to skate; fixing a broken toy; taking us to zoos and amusement parks; treating her to the occasional dinner and dance at the Legion in town. He was so skilled with his hands and he had an intelligent and creative mind.

There was a lot to like. And he was a gentle lover too.

Dad decided that a missing piece in his life was religion and he converted to Catholicism. He became an active participant in the liturgy. Mom didn't have to go to Mass alone anymore.

Yes, there was a lot to like.

There were many questions too. What demons possessed him at times?

Where did they come from?

Why?

From Paris I Came

48

CHAPTER SEVEN
THE LAST DANCE

Dad had a new plan. This one actually made sense. He had found a job as an auditor with Revenue Canada. It would pay significantly more money and it was the break he'd been looking for. However, it required the family move east to Hamilton, Ontario—two hours away from the magical place I had come to love in Ridgetown. Mom understood my distress and did not relish packing again either. She realized her kids would have more opportunity in a big city and our constant financial crisis would finally be ameliorated. Besides the great schools in Hamilton, there were libraries, a thriving steel industry, McMaster University, superior medical and dental care, botanical gardens and other cultural institutions.

Before leaving, we visited Chatham and the farm. Mom learned of a dance being held at Mitchell's Bay—about an hour away from Paincourt. Several family members, including Rita, wanted to go and Dad stayed behind. The band was incredible and her skills returned as if she had been practicing all along. Mom danced with everyone that offered and she moved with almost reckless abandon. At one point, a circle of gyrating revelers formed and she was thrust into the center with the best dancer in the hall. She was flying through an improvised routine and did not want this moment to end.

Mom kept saying to herself, "This is living. This is really living!"

And then it was over. Little did she know it would be her last opportunity to properly dance for the rest of her life.

Exhausted, she returned to the farmhouse and everyone said their goodbyes. Mom had some parting news—she was pregnant again.

The moving van arrived and the Lancaster's were off to Ancaster, Ontario. It was a small village outside Hamilton and Mom and Dad rented on Cumming Court until their big city house was built. Everyone was required to adjust: Dad learned to be an auditor; Ron and I barely tolerated a new school; Sandy made new neighborhood friends and Mom delivered Ken on January 25, 1961. Our family was now complete. There would be no more pregnancies.

It was exciting watching our new house being constructed on Briarwood Crescent. We were all busy in our own way. Mom enjoyed taking Ken and Sandy to a nearby park.

Dad was particularly energized and directed his attention from one passion to another: stamp and coin collecting, golfing, boating, fishing. He introduced us to waterskiing too.

There were occasional trips back to our roots, usually for a funeral. Grandpa Lancaster was the first death that shook us all—it was so sudden. And Dad surprised everyone, from time to time, with another violent outburst or a late night drunken car crash. He was still drinking—heavily at times.

The years flew by and the entire family was putting down new roots in this working class community. We had upgraded to a home on Chateau Court with a ravine and stream in the backyard. Mom was clerking part-time at a women's clothing store and she had her own car—a used, burgundy Plymouth Valiant—with the push button gear-changer feature. Ken was in grade school and enjoying a special relationship with me; Sandy was excelling at Cathedral Girls; Ron had just graduated from Cathedral Boys; I was completing my biology degree and was engaged to be married. And Dad was still raging—from time to time—and several serious incidents with legal ramifications had taken place.

Dad was getting restless and there was an opportunity to work in Ottawa—the capital of Canada—as a government tax consultant. It would mean a big jump in salary, a private office and more prestige. And it would also mean ripping out all those tenderly nurtured roots that had taken the family years to grow.

On looking back, I think Dad was trying to hide and avoid the embarrassment his recent transgressions could have led to. Mom should have said no. She sensed this move would destroy the family.

After much discussion, Mom agreed and off they went in the summer of 1971—Mom, Ron, Sandy and Ken—another fresh start for Dad. I stayed behind to finish my degree and to prepare for my new life with Mary Jo. I had been accepted into McMaster Medical School as well.

It did not take long for everything to unravel at their new home on Fontenay Crescent. Ron lasted one day at Carlton University in Ottawa. He resigned from the program, hurriedly enrolled at McMaster and returned to Hamilton to live with me. It suddenly became crowded in my meagerly appointed second floor apartment.

Dad's drinking escalated and the violence became even more dangerous. One night, he was particularly drunk and lit some newspaper in a wastebasket. Dad placed the flaming container in the stairwell leading to the second floor where the family was sleeping. Mom discovered the fire and extinguished it just in time. The final straw occurred several months later when Dad assaulted Mom and caused serious injuries. He threatened to kill Sandy and Ken too. They sought refuge in a motel and Mom refused the police and medical care. Instead, she called me.

I immediately traveled to Ottawa—a five-hour drive in the middle of the night—and was horrified to see the extent of Mom's injuries. She continued to refuse help and forbade me to call the cops. Sandy and Ken were in a state of shock. I was enraged as I left the motel.

It did not take me long to locate my father and I performed what is now called an intervention. The details of the altercation are not for public consumption. The result of our discussion was the following: Dad never had another drink for the rest of his life; he never lifted a finger to physically hurt Mom or any other family member again; I instructed him to return home and live an honorable life he could be proud of.

All these years later, I am still amazed that Dad actually quit drinking for good that day. If he hadn't, he would have lost me forever.

I returned to the motel and drove Mom, my precious sister and shell-shocked little brother, back to the house. I stayed for several awkward days to reinforce the ground rules.

Dad returned to work and became obsessed with collecting golf memorabilia, club repair and genealogy. He might not have been drinking and flailing around, but still made his noxious presence known. He disowned Sandy because she quit college to live with the love of her life—Marv—a professional football player. And when Mom announced she wanted to return to school and get a better job, he told her she was too stupid to graduate.

Perhaps this was why Mom had followed Dad so far from her original home. She wanted to outlast this man for whom she had lost all respect. He had beaten her, but he was incapable of breaking her spirit. She enrolled in high school classes and brushed off his derogatory comments. Her determination was unmatched.

During this tumultuous time, Mom's father died on January 1, 1972 and the entire family made a harrowing journey—in the middle of winter—back to Paincourt. Family and friends were devastated.

Mom felt nothing and never shed a tear. There was too much water under their broken bridge.

Mom completed her studies, graduated with honors and received three job offers. She accepted a position at Carlton University in the grants department and became proficient using a computer. Dad would show up at her office—unannounced—to start a fight and remind others she was incompetent. A supportive professor wanted to call the police and

Mom waved him off.

In 1981, her beloved sister, Jane, passed away from metastatic breast cancer. The disease ravaged her body but did nothing to diminish her spirit. She was defiant and feisty to the end.

Mom could not stop crying.

She returned to Ottawa to discover that Dad was a depressed and broken person. Ken left to live with me, Mary Jo and our two young kids. He attended McMaster University and found his stride.

The Fontenay Crescent home was now as quiet as a church. Dad had become fearful of the most mundane things. He applied for an early retirement; they purchased an old house in central Hamilton and Mom was happy to be near her children again.

They unpacked and organized their new home at 35 Bowman Street, across from McMaster Medical Center, and became reacquainted with the family—including Sandy, Marv and their children. Mom applied for a job at McMaster, and given her glowing references, she was instantly hired by a professor in need of help with grant applications.

Dad enjoyed his retired status and doted on his many grandchildren. On August 16, 1984 he passed away in his sleep—a heart attack. He was fifty-seven years old. There had been no warning. The preceding afternoon, he helped me build a swing set for the grandkids and once the project was complete, he jumped into the pool and cooled off. He toweled himself dry and waved goodbye forever.

Mom discovered him—lifeless—next to her in bed. I was summoned and arrived a short time later. He was beyond rescue at that point. Because his passing was sudden and unexpected, the police were involved and the coroner was obligated to investigate.

The body was released; visitation and the funeral followed, and his burial was but a formality.

Mom felt nothing. And she never shed a tear.

CHAPTER EIGHT
LOVE LETTERS

She returned to Bowman Street after the burial. Eventually the family left and she was finally alone in the empty house. Mom looked at the pillow on the bed where they had last slept together. It was dented from the weight of Dad's head. She took note of his comb and toothbrush—perfectly placed next to the bathroom sink. He was always so organized.

Mom walked into the living room, sat in a chair and began to appreciate the enormity of the task ahead. Dad had controlled all the money and paid all the bills. She had never been privy to his filing system. Mom was feeling a little panicky about her financial future, and then remembered he had been receiving a sizable pension from Revenue Canada that would be redirected to her. Their home was paid for and she had a job at McMaster.

Mom had never experienced anything like this. She knew there would be lots of agencies and institutions to contact, but she didn't know which ones to call and there was no list of phone numbers to guide her.

She wondered how her kids were coping and thought about having a drink. And then a vision popped into her head. It did not last for more than a moment. It was of Doug, jumping from the cherry tree—goofy and drunk—and asking her for a dance. What ever happened to him? In his final seconds, he didn't even put up a fight.

Mom did have that drink and slept well all night. She awoke refreshed and started composing her to-do list. She called the lawyer and made an appointment. There were frequent phone interruptions—calls from her children. They visited every day and helped dispose of Dad's personal items. His clothes were donated to the poor, the genealogy project was boxed and stored for another day, his historical golf books and artifacts were gifted to Golf Canada and the kids kept several mementos.

These tasks were an almost welcome distraction from something called self-doubt that was whispering in her ear. It was reminding her she had never lived alone. Mom had no idea what it would be like to organize a schedule that was not dictated by someone else's demands. And how would she cope with the silence?

Years ago when I was recording our conversations, Mom told me that she knew she was strong and had endured many things. However, the few months after Dad died were the most stressful of her life. She wasn't certain who she was and could not see a path forward. "It was really hard," she said.

It was a blessing she had a job to return to. Her coworkers were a great support and the projects took her mind off things. Work provided some necessary structure at the time.

And then I came along with a new proposition. I asked Mom if she would consider working as a receptionist at my Upper James Street office. I knew her dream, abandoned long ago, was to be a nurse. Now she could be around patients and become part of their extended family as we helped them with their medical issues. Mom was caring, calm under pressure, organized, punctual and had the ability to be firm but pleasant. She definitely had the correct skills to excel at this job.

I informed her that Sandy was going to work at the office too. She would schedule specialist appointments and file lab results. And Mary Jo was starting as the office manager, now that our children were all in school. It would be a real family run business.

Mom realized I could not match McMaster's pay scale and benefit package. She didn't care about that. Mom jumped at the idea of working with me.

All the patients became aware she was my mother. And they revered her and knew she was doing her best to get them the earliest appointment. They appreciated her calming voice and the wisdom that comes from having been the mother of four children. She called me Dr. Lancaster at work. My patients called me Dr. Bob.

Mom loved the drama of having to cancel and rebook patients because "the doctor had a delivery" or "surgery was running late."

One day, she actually became part of the

drama. A man she had never met burst into the office, yelled that his wife was in labor and pleaded for help. The couple had been on their way to the hospital and realized they wouldn't make it—the baby was coming too fast. They had seen my office sign, took a chance and pulled into the lot. He was frantic.

Mom pulled me out of an exam room and we raced to a car parked cock-eyed near the entrance door. A pregnant woman was in the back seat, naked from the waist down, and she was in an advanced stage of labor. Mom appeared with a wheelchair and once inside an examination room, we lifted the panting lady onto the table. I hurriedly gathered some instruments—I did home births on occasion—and Mom gathered towels, sheets and boiled the proverbial water.

Both Sandy and Mom fetched whatever was needed. The reception area became a labor and delivery waiting room as patients arrived for appointments and were caught-up in the excitement. Everyone held their collective breath and then they heard a cry—tiny at first—and then a full-throated scream.

I could hear applause coming from the waiting room. I peeked out the door and everyone was standing and clapping. "It's a boy," I said. My mother was beaming. You would have thought it was her grandson. She was so proud of me and how I had performed during this crisis. It was the best day of her entire work career.

The new father insisted on taking photos of everyone involved. About an hour later, while I was seeing patients, the healthy baby and happy mother left my office. Mom and Sandy helped them to their car. The new mom had not required stitches and they never did go to the hospital.

The husband returned the next day with flowers for Mom and Sandy too. They lived out of town, we didn't have their insurance information and it wasn't worth the hassle of trying to bill them. I had been more than paid with their gratitude.

And so it went. My mother thrived as the receptionist.

Of course she was not just proud of me. She admired all her children and was in awe of their accomplishments. Mom had bragging rights when she compared her kids with her nieces and nephews. I'm sure she never boasted because it was not her nature. But she would have liked to.

We all enjoyed doing special things with Mom and treated her to restaurants, plays, concerts, movies and taking her on family trips. She loved to spend time babysitting her many grandchildren too.

Mary Jo and I invited her on several family vacations. We visited Myrtle Beach where she saw the Atlantic Ocean for the first time. Mom was so excited that she ran into the water—fully clothed—only to be chased back by an incoming wave.

Mom also enjoyed visiting Disneyworld and Canada's Wonderland, cruising to Mexico, visiting Taos and the Pueblo during their holy season, sightseeing in Sedona, camping at the Grand Canyon and house boating on Lake Powell.

She snorkeled for the first and only time during a family vacation in Maui. While there, Mom and I took a day trip to Oahu while Mary Jo and the kids stayed behind at the resort. I drove her to all the places Dad had written about in his love letters so many years before. He had been stationed there during the war. Mom gazed out from Pali Lookout at the same spot he had taken photos from. She saw Diamond Head, Kolekole pass and the Dole pineapple fields. I gained entrance to Schofield Barracks, and she choked up when she saw the church where Dad had prayed for strength. He had asked to be spared and make it home—back to her waiting arms.

Why had she burned those letters?

What was she thinking?

Mom felt she was born to be a mother and devoted her entire life to initially nurturing and protecting, and later educating and supporting us all. Ron, Sandy, Ken and I are her crowning achievements. She heaps praise on us and celebrates our every success.

However, she always assumes complete responsibility when we have a health problem or a personal setback. "Perhaps it's something I ate while I was pregnant," she says. "Maybe I could have been more helpful or given better advice."

Sometimes she laments she should have left Dad in order to remove us from his violence and keep us safe. On one occasion, I pushed the conversation and asked why she hadn't left. Mom said it was complicated. She had nowhere to go, and women's shelters were not being built yet. She had no money and it was doubtful Dad would have paid child support. If she had called the police and tried to escape, Mom was convinced he would have killed her.

She did turn to her father, but he refused to help. He wrote her off with the words, "you made your bed—go lay in it," or sentiments to that effect. Her sisters were overwhelmed with their rapidly growing families, their own financial woes and were not in a position to help.

Mom hoped Dad would learn to control his anger and curtail his drinking. When he was sober, he was a wonderful father and loving spouse. Unfortunately, he never did seriously seek help and his violent explosions continued to happen.

We've talked about her not leaving many times. She has observed that modern women stand up against abuse and other injustices and Mom is embarrassed that she was not as brave. I've reminded her that the world has changed. There are now shelters, counselors, anger management classes, Alcoholics Anonymous, more comprehensive laws, better trained police, a more responsive court system, self-help books and on and on.

She nods her head in agreement after these pep talks, and then continues to second guess her actions.

It appears Mom is seeking forgiveness for something she didn't do wrong. Life is challenging enough, and the guilt she drags around like an anchor makes her journey that much more difficult.

From Paris I Came

CHAPTER NINE
THE GAZEBO

Living on Bowman Street had become problematic for Mom. There was a front and back yard to mow, flower beds to maintain and bushes to trim. Winter brought the new challenge of snow removal from the sidewalk and driveway. The house itself was old and in need of repairs. Many surrounding properties were being repurposed as student housing for the university across the street. It was not the same quiet neighborhood anymore.

Mom was now in her late sixties and lonely. She had lost her mother in October, 1989. She was eighty-five years old and unable to recover from emergency abdominal surgery. They had remained emotionally close even though distance had kept them apart for more than three decades.

The farm and the bulk of the estate were willed to her brother, Gerry. The two surviving sisters, Rita and Mom, were hurt. They had been omitted from the will. To add further insult, they were required to purchase nostalgic items they wanted from the estate. Their hard work toiling in the fields when they were young went unrecognized and uncompensated.

Mom had to cope with another loss. In 1991, I moved my family to Arizona seeking greener pastures. And up until that point, I'd been doing her landscaping.

She was also busy helping Ron, Sandy, and eventually me, cope with the aftermath of failed relationships.

All three of us experienced painful divorces. Thankfully, they were not all at the same time, for Mom's sake. Of course she felt responsible, because she assumed our personal problems were caused by traumatic childhoods. We navigated the awkwardness of introducing her to our new loves.

And then Gerry passed away in 1999 from complications related to cancer. Of course, Mom was sad. However, it was the death of her beloved sister, Jane, many years before that still left the biggest hole in her heart.

Getting back to Bowman Street, Mom was trying to decide what to do about the mounting issues related to home ownership. It was at that moment of uncertainty when Ken and his wife, Deb, stepped forward with an exciting idea. They asked Mom if she would consider living with them.

This made sense for so many reasons. Mom could sell her house, invest the bulk of the proceeds and put the trials and tribulations of home ownership behind her. She would be in a secure setting and enjoy being part of a young family, complete with grandchildren. After all, Michael and the twins—Cam and Chris—were preschoolers and a joy to be around.

 It was emphasized that Ken and Deb would assist her as she inevitably aged. This was a comforting thought. Mom would also be helping them with the cost of home ownership and enjoy an equity position too.

Mom liked the idea of knowing she was helping her youngest child. And the thought of being part of her grandchildren's lives was tantalizing. She took her time, sought other opinions, weighed everything carefully and called Ken.

"I'd love to be part of your family," she said. A new chapter in their lives had begun.

Once she moved in, it was impossible not to notice the added spring in Mom's step. The grandkids had rejuvenated her. She was so pleased with the arrangement that she bought a gazebo for her side yard. She was putting down roots. I recall landscaping around this enchanting outdoor sitting area, utilizing every conceivable perennial plant to ensure color in the spring, summer and fall. My new wife, Lucy, assisted in the planting and we were pleased with the result, as was Mom.

I enjoyed staying at her ground floor suite when I visited from Arizona. As an added bonus, I got to see Ken's family too. Mom lived there for many happy years.

Grandchildren grow up, situations change and mom pined for more privacy. She still desired a secure setting, but wanted to be near people her age. Mom yearned to play cards, socialize and maybe even dance again.

She chose a condominium in Dundas, Ontario, not far from her children—other than me. The building was occupied by seniors and required a code to enter. It was within walking distance of a Catholic church and close to numerous shops that lined the main street.

Leaving anything behind is always bitter-sweet. And trying something new is a calculated risk. Mom packed her things, looked in the mirror at her now wrinkled face, smoothed her hair and walked as upright as possible to her waiting Toyota.

The moment reminded her of leaving the farm many years ago to live with the Wests.

She had flashbacks of sharing the space with Uncle Goldie's demented father, where he spewed chewing tobacco in all directions. Thank goodness she was not returning there.

Once is enough for many things in life.

CHAPTER TEN
DICKENS

With all due respect to Charles Dickens, the Dundas years for Mom were the best of times and the worst of times.

Her condominium was located in the heart of town. She did make new friends and attended the Senior Center, where she resurrected her old card playing skills. She loved the quiet of her new space. Mom met other condo owners and enjoyed their regular get-togethers. She became well known by the shop owners up and down the main street. Mom could walk to the Catholic Church only three blocks away. She felt secure in the building and had a convenient underground parking spot for her old but reliable Toyota.

When I visited Dundas, one of her favorite things to do was hike with me along a trail beside Spencer Creek. She was thrilled to be out in nature again: marveling at the spring flowers, identifying the many birds, and observing the fresh water salmon run in the fall.

It was after one of those walks that I sat down on her living room couch and finally told her about me—I was transgender.

Mom was confused. She had never heard of such a thing, and our subsequent conversations could be the topic for another book. In the end, it was not difficult for her to accept me because she loved me. Mom and I have moved forward, mangled pronouns and all.

While I'm on the topic of acceptance, I must point out that Mom, like all of us, has met many different people during the course of her life. By nature, she is wary of strangers and this could be misinterpreted as being prejudiced. She gives everyone a chance to reveal their character and if they are good people, she can be the most welcoming person in the room. "It's what's in their heart that matters, and not where they're from or the color of their skin," she says.

However, there are some things that really do upset her, like political correctness. Or someone looking for a handout, but being unwilling to work.

Getting back to life in Dundas, Mom started a family tradition that has continued to this day. Every time I visited from Arizona, she treated the family to an upper-end restaurant called Shakespeare's. This was the highlight of my twice a year trips. She loved indulging her kids even though she was on a fixed income. At the end of the meal, she made certain she had received her money's worth by secretly filling her purse from the big bowl of candy offered for dessert.

There were some not-so-nice things that Mom experienced living in Dundas. The peace and quiet was often shattered by emergency vehicle sirens—a police station was around the corner. The idyllic main street was often closed for rambunctious festivals, complete with late night concerts. Drunken patrons would regularly stumble out of the taverns in the wee hours after closing, talking loudly as they staggered below her condo window and down the road. And why did the library across the street have to leave its lights on all night, illuminating her bedroom?

And then there was Chuck. He was a few years older than Mom and he was divorced, or so he told her. His former wife, he explained, was a mental case.

Mom met him at the senior center where he served on the board. He was handsome, a persuasive talker and he played golf. He reminded her of someone she knew a long time ago.

Mom enjoyed having a close friend again. They went hiking on the local trails and enjoyed every restaurant in the vicinity. He fancied himself to be a photographer and his favorite subject was Mom. Of course she was flattered. She introduced Chuck to the family and we greeted him in a friendly manner. However, our collective guard was up. Mom played down the significance of the friendship.

Behind the scenes, he was pressing her for intimacy and talking about marriage. They went on several road trips together that ended in arguments and when the relationship appeared over, he was back again. Chuck told her that she was the only love of his life and bought her many Royal Dalton figurines. Mom reassured us she could handle the situation.

More information trickled in. We learned he was a recovering alcoholic who was, for the most part, estranged from his family. However, he had attended Alcoholics Anonymous meetings weekly for several decades and further redeemed himself by mentoring new members. Mom told me he managed his money poorly and lived pension check to pension check.

There was one more thing: he wasn't actually divorced. If he had severed legal ties, he explained, his wife would have lost the benefit of being covered by his health insurance. Things were sounding fishier every day.

One day, we heard the bomb-shell news. Chuck's wife had been murdered. It made the headlines in the local newspaper and sent shock waves through our family. The killer was still on the loose. Over the next few months, many interviews, tips and forensic analyses took place. The murderer could not be found.

Chuck was now free to marry.

The last thing on Mom's mind was marriage. It would mean giving up Dad's pension and she was not stupid.

Mom had other concerns. She had developed significant orthopedic problems necessitating knee and hip replacements. Her rehabilitation was slow and was compromised by the limited movement of her shoulders and neck. All of the past farm work and a lifetime of wear and tear had taken its toll. She was also developing word finding difficulties and her thinking had slipped a notch too.

Chuck visited frequently during her recovery until he became sick himself. It was cancer, and now it was Mom's turn to visit him at his apartment.

His decline gathered speed. It was there that she learned he had been seeing another woman during the entire time he had been romancing her.

The news cut her like a knife. She had experienced this kind of betrayal before, and it was even more crushing now.

How could she have been so trusting? Mom continued to visit him until his last breath at a hospice facility. She did it out of obligation.

Mom felt nothing after he died.

And then she had to endure the accusations of his daughter, who thought Mom might be harboring some of her father's money.

There would be no more men in Mom's life ever again. She firmly closed that door and threw away the key to her heart.

Life in Dundas had become depressing. Most of her friends from the Community Center had become institutionalized or had died. Even her neighbors in the condo had passed away. There was literally a funeral a week. Mom attempted to meet new people and continue to play cards. However, they were all younger, sharper and played quickly. She felt rushed and made mistakes that her bid-euchre partner did not appreciate.

She quit going to cards.

Her driving skills were deteriorating too.

Initially Mom hid the truth from herself. However, she did not want to have an accident or hurt someone. She relinquished her license, sold the car to her grandson and bought a walker.

Mom discovered that there was a definite downside to a long life. She felt like she was mourning all the time because there was something or someone being lost daily. Her friends and original family were all gone, except for Rita who lived far away and was hard of hearing. Their phone conversations were difficult.

Mom was losing weight and was diagnosed with a slow-growing lymphoma. She was throwing out food that she did not feel like eating, and there was no one to share a meal with anyway.

She told me she was not ready to leave her family. She was not ready to die and wanted to fight.

Mom prayed to God to give her strength. It was time for a new plan.

CHAPTER ELEVEN
UNBREAKABLE

I originally had intended to write a short essay about my mother, Rosalie, and how much she loved to dance. It would have been fun to share with her and my siblings. And then I got carried away. I came to realize that she has an incredible life story and it became my responsibility to tell it.

Can you imagine being born into poverty in rural Ontario during the Great Depression, and being rejected by your father because you weren't a boy? And never having your farm work acknowledged, even though you did as much as any son could have done?

And can you imagine a parent who would prevent a child from continuing their education, even when the cost was going to be covered by another relative? The implications were life-altering. If it wasn't for the love she received from a strong woman—her Memere Belanger—I think Rosalie could have been a lost soul.

The power of a supportive mentor cannot be overstated. It allowed Rosalie to blossom and reach for things that seemed impossible. She won a best actress award for portraying Joan of Arc in a school play and her confidence grew. Once she discovered something deep inside called self-belief, Rosalie was equipped to push back against the discrimination she experienced because she was French and command attention on the dance floor as everyone looked on in admiration.

These experiences made her a more effective wife and mother too. It allowed her to stand tall and persevere, no matter what curve balls life threw at her.

Take a peek at her now as she starts a new chapter at a senior living facility. You are looking at a survivor—a ninety year old warrior—who is not scared to fail, and who is willing to try something new. She carries on because she loves her family and wants to continue to enjoy their company and help them along their way. If you expect to see her break, you might as well leave now because it is not going to happen.

Mom traveled to Arizona several months ago with Sandy. It was a long time in the planning stage and no easy feat.

She wanted to enjoy our desert oasis one last time. Mom hoped she would witness the desert in bloom. However, she did not want to see any rattlesnakes.

She insisted I take her to Boyce Thompson Arboretum where I lead general tours. Once there, Mom became energized and had to see the whole park, especially the canyon. Take a look at the photo below. You are observing determination in action as she negotiates the switchbacks on her way to the riparian area below.

Finally, I'd like to say a word about several individuals in the book who could easily be called villains. Nothing could be farther from the truth. There was no malice in their hearts: their behavior was basically pre-programmed. Let me explain. They were the products of their genetics and the parenting—or lack of—that they received. Some experts call it poisoned pedagogy. They reflected the norms and the thinking of the times. And perhaps they were never fortunate enough to have had a mentor: someone older and wiser who could have given them the gift of confidence and shown them a different path forward.

I have always loved my mother. However, after writing this book, I've developed an even deeper admiration and respect for her. My wish is that she will have the opportunity to dance again someday.

After all, from Paris she came, and Rosalie is her name.

ABOUT THE AUTHOR

Bobbi lives in Gold Canyon, Arizona and is a family physician, author, speaker and transgender rights advocate. She also enjoyed a brief career as a professional golfer.

She is the proud parent of three incredible children and is thrilled to have two talented grandchildren as well. Bobbi is happily married to Lucy, a nurse practitioner, who shares the same passion for helping people. Lucy is also an AKC Breeder of Merit who takes pride in the quality of her Havanese puppies. Bobbi supports her hobby and serves as the principle poop-scooper. This literally keeps her grounded.

Bobbi currently volunteers as a docent at Boyce Thompson Arboretum where she leads general tours and enjoys connecting the public with nature in a profound way. She also serves on the board of directors of this cherished old park.

She can be reached at the following: plusoneatsixty@hotmail.com.

From Paris I Came

94

THANKS

Writing this book is the result of an impulse that came over me about five weeks before my mother's ninetieth birthday. I want it to be a surprise.

This rushed project required the help of many. Ron, Sandy and Ken searched their photo albums and supplied me with pictures. Lucy provided her proof-reading skills.

I did enlist the help of a professional— Jackie Casey—an illustrator extraordinaire. She formatted the book, designed the cover and sent it off to the publisher.

Everyone became caught up in this labor of love and many hands made light work. There is nothing I can say or do to adequately thank them all.

I love you guys.
Bobbi